RHYTHM OF
SUCCESS

Exploring the Impact of Verbal and Nonverbal
Communication in Social Media and
Face-to-Face Encounters

Giulio Veglio

DEDICATION

This book is a tribute to the countless individuals who have significantly influenced my journey, offering their support, love, guidance, and steadfast belief in me. These pillars have been crucial in my personal and professional growth.

First and foremost, I express my deepest gratitude to God for blessing me with unlimited gifts to open and share. It is through His grace that I have been able to embark on this path and make a positive impact in the lives around me.

To my mentors, each of you holds a special place in my heart. Your wisdom, guidance, and unwavering support have been invaluable. Through sharing your knowledge and experiences, you have helped me to navigate life's hurdles and embrace the opportunities that have arisen. Your faith in my abilities has been a constant source of encouragement.

To my mother and father, thank you for your unconditional love, mentoring, discipline, and guidance. You have instilled in me the values of integrity and honesty, shaping the person I am today. Your unwavering support has been the bedrock of my achievements.

To my brother, Dr. G, and my sisters, Elvira and Maria, thank you for always looking out for me and caring for my well-being. Your presence in my life has brought joy, laughter, and a sense of belonging. I cherish our bond and the strength we derive from each other.

To my wife, Ashley, you are my rock and my biggest supporter. Your love, encouragement, and unwavering belief in me have fueled my determination to pursue my dreams. Thank you for being by my side through thick and thin and blessing me with our beautiful baby girl, Evangelina.

To my two boys, Giulio Jr. and Stefano. You both are the driving force behind my purpose and the embodiment of our love.

This book is dedicated to all those who have touched my life, directly or indirectly. Your presence, love, and support have made all the difference. This book embodies the essence of gratitude, love, and the conviction that, surrounded by the right individuals, we are capable of achieving greatness.

ABOUT THE AUTHOR

Giulio Veglio is a seasoned business professional, author, and philanthropist with a rich background in business startup and development, team leadership, and client relations. He is a certified Behavior Analysis Trainer and Consultant and a certified Maxwell Leadership, Executive, Trainer, Speaker, and Coach.

Veglio's educational background is extensive, with an Executive MBA from Harvard Business School and certifications from the Florida Department of Law Enforcement, Seminole County Sheriff's Office, and Johns Hopkins University, among others. He is also an ordained minister from the Universal Life Church.

Veglio's professional journey began in 1984 with John Paul Mitchell Systems / Paul Mitchell the School, where he started as an independent hair salon owner/operator and later became an educator, master, and member of the Special Task Force. He has been instrumental in developing and implementing customer service and efficiency systems and has managed multiple locations across various states.

Veglio's achievements are numerous, including the 2023 Outstanding Leadership Award by International Education 2.0, the Paul Mitchell Schools National Excellence in Operations Business Award (2022), and the Visionary Media - Philanthropist of the Year

(2019) and Lifetime Achievement Award (2019), among others. He is also a multi-award published author!

In addition to his professional accomplishments, Veglio is a dedicated philanthropist, helping to raise over $25M annually for various charities. He is bilingual, speaking both English and Italian, and is a proud Italian immigrant who received U.S. citizenship in 1974.

CONTENTS

INTRODUCTION

I'm here to share a lifelong dream of mine—one that I believe will make you more successful and pave the way for your success in the ever-evolving world. What's the secret sauce, you ask? It's all about the art of customer service, and it's a game-changer from the moment your clients set foot in your salon until they bid farewell.

Building a good relationship with clients is also one of the secret sauces nowadays; creating perfect social media accounts with outstanding marketing of the services provided is also the ideal or – the only sauce you need to expand your business. I speak from over two decades of experience in this active industry, and my passion for it has never diminished since day one.

When I first stepped into hairstyling, I instantly fell in love with it. But my steady focus on my financial prosperity set me on the path to success. Everyone has that one common goal—to make money, which reflects our dedication and expertise in the field.

So, let's get on this journey together, equipped with modern strategies that will revolutionize your career, boost your clientele, and open doors to exciting opportunities in chemical services and product sales. Our ultimate goal is to be successful, but it's important to shift our focus towards the actionable steps that lead us there, enabling us to boost our income and rise to the pinnacle of excellence in the service industry. I've had the privilege of collaborating with some of the industry's luminaries, soaking up invaluable insights I'm eager to share.

When I first began my hairstyling journey, I believed improving my technical skills was the key to success. I invested heavily in perfecting my hair cutting, chemical relaxation, updo, and perm techniques.

I traveled through the globe, from New York to California and from London to Paris and Italy, all in the search for technical excellence. It was a considerable investment in terms of both money and time.

However, my perspective changed when I became part of the John Paul Mitchell Systems community. I discovered that true success in today's business world extends beyond technical ability—it's about mastering the art of marketing through social media. This paradigm shift has been transformative, and it's the game-changer that I'm eager to explore with you.

When I realized the pivotal role of social media marketing in our industry, I shifted my focus. As I revisited the lessons from these esteemed masters, I carefully observed their strategies and identified a crucial element that made them stand out. It wasn't solely their technical expertise; it was the exceptional way they engaged with their audience, from the moment they initiated an online connection to the final interaction. This comprehensive approach was the true key to their remarkable success in the work of social media marketing.

This timeless principle remains as relevant as ever in our modern world of the services era. I'm excited to guide you on this transformative journey so you, too, can attain the same level of success as these legendary masters, all while keeping pace with the contemporary demands of our industry.

During the COVID-19 pandemic, many businesses faced significant challenges. In April 2020, hair salon visits declined by 60% due to government-mandated closures and social distancing measures. Although 2020 was a tough year for everyone, 2021 saw some recovery as vaccines became available and restrictions eased, leading to increased revenue in the salon industry.

However, post-COVID-19, Many companies adopted new strategies beyond their traditional focus on excellent customer service.

I've studied many successful businesses and noticed that they did something different than just their technical skills in every step they took. I studied how they handled their social media platforms and how they dealt with the customers from the moment they walked into the door or logged in on Social Media platforms to the moment they personally left or logged off from Social Media and how it made them successful.

I want to take you on that journey so that you, too, can be as successful as all those other people and all those great masters out there.

Imagine that you have to plan out a dinner, and you're trying to look out for good restaurants. As you scroll through the phone, eyes searching for the perfect restaurant, you look at various options and consider flavor, ambiance, and good food. Each swipe presents a range of culinary options, providing a distinct dining experience in taste and atmosphere.

However, as you click on one of the restaurants that caught your eye, you find yourself drawn into the delectable content they've shared on their social media account. Scrolling through their tempting posts, you stumble upon the *"Reviews"* section. Out of curiosity, you tap it, only to be greeted by many less-than-glowing reviews about its ambiance, customer service, and even the quality of its food.

With a casual shrug and a touch of disappointment, your eyes skim through the critical comments. After absorbing the less-than-ideal feedback, you close the page, and the discouraging reviews slightly deflate your dining plans.

You, again, begin your search for the perfect restaurant, and finally, you come across the restaurant you were looking for. You open their page and review their feed, menu, and reviews. As you review their studies, you find yourself satisfied and happy with the number of good reviews regarding customer service, ambiance, and food.

Indeed, it's clear that you're going to visit the restaurant with positive reviews. Likewise, in this era of widespread social media and advanced technology, how people approach their choices has evolved significantly. Individuals increasingly turn to the internet's vast resources for information before visiting a particular place, be it a restaurant, a shop, or any other establishment.

They set out on a digital adventure, scrolling through reviews, pictures, and posts on various social media platforms. It's become a crucial part of how they decide where to go. They're more likely to plan a visit if they vibe with a place's online presence, see some thumbs-up reviews, and stumble upon exciting content that matches their interests.

In this digital era, how businesses show up online and how potential customers perceive them in the virtual world can make a big difference in drawing people in and ensuring success. It's a friendly nudge to remind us all of the importance of keeping a positive and engaging online presence to capture the attention and trust of today's discerning consumers.

Consider this: an impressive thirty-eight percent of communication impact is attributed to voice inflection. The way you modulate your tone and utilize your voice can significantly express confidence or reveal a lack thereof. Recall the memorable "Seinfeld" episode featuring the puffy shirt?

In that episode, the character couldn't hear what the girl was saying and mindlessly agreed with her, leading to a situation where he had to wear an embarrassing shirt on a T.V. show. This shows how miscommunication can have consequences and applies to conditions like dealing with clients or social media interactions. It underscores the importance of clear, confident communication to prevent misunderstandings and conflicts. Whether chatting with someone in person or asking a question online, being straightforward and self-assured can help you avoid awkward or problematic situations caused by miscommunication.

Now, here's the kicker: a staggering fifty-eight percent is influenced by non-verbal communication. Much like the restaurant's page you left, which lost its appeal after reading the reviews, more than half of what people perceive is connected to non-verbal cues—such as the appearance of the place, your presentation, your demeanor, and the overall ambiance. Let's examine how these non-verbal elements impact the client experience as we navigate our salon.

There are instances where a business's social media marketing appears to be exceptional. Everyone seems excited to visit, but the experience is disappointing. Business entrepreneurs must grasp that if their social media performance is outstanding, their customer service must match that level of excellence. A strong social media presence loses its value if it doesn't result in satisfied and loyal customers.

If you're considering opening any business, it's important to ensure that your social media strategy and customer service are outstanding. This way, when you attract new customers who plan to revisit, they will be more likely to share positive reviews on your social media platform and with their friends, helping to build your reputation and attract even more customers to your business.

I want to share some of the tips I've learned from my experience in this industry so that you can gain valuable insights and improve your business!

CHAPTER 1

FROM PIXELS TO HANDSHAKES:

NAVIGATING FIRST IMPRESSIONS IN THE DIGITAL AGE

In a world where our lives are increasingly intertwined with technology, how we connect and communicate has undergone a profound transformation. The rise of social media platforms has ushered in a new era of introductions, where first impressions are formed through verbal and nonverbal cues experienced in the virtual realm. As we explore this digital landscape, we question how our online personas align with our real-life selves. How do we ensure consistency between the impressions we make online and those we make face-to-face? In this book, we delve into the fascinating evolution of first impressions, exploring the nuances of both past and present, and discover practical strategies to maintain authenticity and cohesion as we transition from the virtual to the physical world.

1. The Power of In-Person Introductions

Once upon a time, introductions were made through direct human interaction, where handshakes, eye contact, and body language played pivotal roles. We relied on these tangible cues to form impressions, gauging a person's character and trustworthiness. The spoken word, accompanied by facial expressions and gestures, conveyed subtle nuances that shaped our perceptions. We understood the gravity of these initial encounters as they set the tone for future relationships. However, as technology advanced, the landscape of introductions underwent a seismic shift.

2. The Dawn of the Digital Era

With the advent of social media, a new dimension emerged, blending the personal and the virtual. Suddenly, we found ourselves crafting online profiles, meticulously curating images, and selecting words to encapsulate our identities. This book explores social media's impact on forming first impressions. We examine the power of words, the influence of visuals, and the challenges of deciphering authenticity in a world of filtered experiences. How do we ensure that our virtual introductions remain true to who we are?

3. Navigating the Detail Landscape

As we immerse ourselves in the vast and intricate realm of social media, it becomes imperative to maintain consistency in our online presence. This book discusses strategies to cultivate authenticity despite the pressures of a curated digital world. From aligning our values with our online interactions to developing a personal brand that accurately reflects our true selves, we explore techniques to bridge the gap between the virtual and the real.

4. Unveiling the Authentic Self

The time comes when we must transition from pixels to handshakes, from virtual interactions to face-to-face encounters. This book examines the challenges of merging our online and offline personas. We explore the importance of congruence between verbal and nonverbal cues, emphasizing the significance of body language, tone of voice, and eye contact in making a lasting impression. How can we ensure that the person we present is consistent with the person we projected online?

To be honest, I still prefer personal interactions rather than online interactions. However, times have changed, and we must adapt to these changes.

Conclusion:

We will embark on a journey to understand the evolving nature of introductions. We will unravel the complexities of virtual connections, exploring the power of social media to shape perceptions. We will uncover strategies to maintain consistency, authenticity, and coherence as we transition from digital to genuine human encounters. Join us as we navigate this transformative landscape, empowering ourselves to make meaningful online and offline connections.

CHAPTER 2

THE GREETING

In a world where communication is increasingly digital, it is essential to recognize the significance of greetings in both verbal and non-verbal interactions. Greetings are the foundation for establishing connections, setting the tone, and conveying respect and warmth. Whether through social media platforms or face-to-face encounters, understanding the importance of greetings can significantly enhance our communication skills. Here, we will explore the power of greetings and their key points in various communication contexts and provide exercises to practice effective greetings.

The Power of Greetings:

> *"Every interaction starts with a greeting, and it sets the stage for the entire conversation."*
>
> – Unknown

Greeting someone, whether online or in person, is the first step towards building rapport and establishing a positive atmosphere. It shows respect, acknowledges the other person's presence, and creates a welcoming environment. Greetings can make someone feel valued and appreciated, leading to more meaningful and productive interactions.

Once upon a time, I was surrounded by a melting pot of cultures in the vibrant city of Schenectady, New York. Growing up as an immigrant in this diverse community exposed me to people from all walks of life, each with unique dialects and languages.

While this cultural tapestry enriched my life, it also presented challenges, particularly regarding communication and greetings.

In my early years, my grasp of the English language was limited, and I often found myself using phrases and words that didn't quite exist in the English dictionary. My first attempt at greeting others was a prime example of this linguistic mishmash. Instead of saying *"Hello,"* I would blurt out, *"How ya doin?"*

My vocabulary was peppered with phrases like *"brang"* instead of *"brought"* and *"anit"* instead of *"isn't it."* It was a jumble of words that reflected my upbringing and the cultural influences around me.

Unfortunately, my unconventional greetings were met with mixed reactions. Some people found them endearing, while others perceived them as a lack of education or rudeness. It became clear to me that if I wanted to succeed in the professional world, I needed to refine my greetings and learn the art of proper communication.

Determined to overcome this obstacle, I embarked on a journey of self-improvement. I sought guidance from mentors, enrolled in language courses, and immersed myself in literature to expand my vocabulary. I practiced enunciating words and phrases, paying close attention to pronunciation and intonation. It was a challenging process, but I was determined to master the art of professional greetings.

As I began my career, I put my newfound knowledge into practice. I confidently greeted colleagues and clients, using appropriate phrases such as *"Good morning"* or *"Nice to meet you."* I listened to non-verbal cues, maintaining eye contact and offering a warm smile.

Slowly but surely, I noticed a change in how people perceived me. They no longer saw me as uneducated or rude but rather as someone who had made an effort to adapt and grow.

I engaged in role-playing exercises with friends and colleagues to refine my skills further. We simulated various professional scenarios, focusing on greetings and communication. These exercises allowed me to fine-tune my approach, ensuring my greetings were polite and culturally sensitive.

Through perseverance and a genuine desire to connect with others, I transformed my initial struggles into strengths. I learned that greetings are not just words but bridges connecting individuals and fostering understanding. By embracing the diversity around me and adapting my greetings to different cultural contexts, I built stronger relationships and created a more inclusive environment.

Ultimately, my journey to learn professional greetings taught me a valuable lesson: communication is a powerful tool that can break down barriers and bring people together. Through understanding and respect, we can truly appreciate the richness of our diverse world. So, let us greet one another with open hearts and open minds, celebrating our differences and embracing the beauty of cultural diversity.

Key Points in Greetings through Social Media:

1. Personalized Messages: When initiating conversations on social media platforms, take the time to craft personalized greetings. Address the person by their name and show genuine interest in connecting with them.

2. Tone and Emojis: Use appropriate tone and emojis to convey warmth and friendliness. Emoticons can add a touch of emotion and help bridge the gap created by the absence of non-verbal cues. Be aware of the Emojis you send. There was a time when I made the mistake of using an Emoji, which I thought would create a laugh, but instead, I offended them greatly.

I guess some people do not take kindly to poop Emojis. When I expressed how I felt about the day, they thought I was talking about how I felt about them. Oops!

3. Timeliness: Respond promptly to messages and comments to show that you value the other person's time and engagement. Delayed responses can create a sense of disinterest or neglect.

Key Points in Greetings in In-Person Verbal and Non-Verbal Interaction:

1. Eye Contact and Smile: Make eye contact and offer a warm smile when greeting someone in person—this non-verbal communication signals openness and approachability.

2. Handshakes and Hugs: Depending on cultural norms and the level of familiarity, handshakes or hugs can be appropriate greetings. Pay attention to the other person's cues and adjust accordingly.

3. Vocal Tone and Body Language: Use a friendly and welcoming vocal tone and open body language to convey sincerity and interest. Avoid crossing arms or displaying closed-off postures.

<u>Exercises to Practice Effective Greetings:</u>

1. Social Media Greeting Challenge: Reach out to five individuals on social media platforms and initiate conversations with personalized greetings. Observe their responses and note the impact of your greetings on the overall interaction.

2. In-Person Greeting Role Play: Pair up with a friend or colleague and take turns practicing greetings in various scenarios. Focus on maintaining eye contact, using appropriate body language, and delivering warm vocal tones.

Main Idea:

Effective greetings are the cornerstone of successful communication, both online and offline. They set the tone, establish rapport, and create a positive atmosphere for meaningful interactions. By mastering the art of greetings, we can enhance our communication skills and build stronger connections with others.

Conclusion:

In a world where communication is evolving rapidly, the importance of greetings remains constant. Whether through social media or in-person interactions, greetings play a vital role in establishing connections and fostering positive relationships.

By understanding the key points of greetings and practicing them through exercises, we can harness the power of greetings to create more meaningful and impactful communication experiences. Remember, a simple greeting can make a lasting impression and open doors to endless possibilities.

CHAPTER 3

THE POWER OF CONSULTATION:

VERBAL AND NON-VERBAL ACTIONS IN SOCIAL MEDIA AND IN-PERSON INTERACTIONS

"Effective communication begins with mutual respect, communication that inspires and encourages others to do their best."

- Zig Ziglar

Verbal communication is not just about making statements; it's also about asking questions and providing positive feedback. Questions can stimulate thought, provoke curiosity, and encourage dialogue. As Roy T. Bennett once said, *"Listen with curiosity. Speak with honesty. Act with integrity."* Positive feedback, on the other hand, can boost morale, foster a positive environment, and encourage continuous improvement.

In a business context, suggesting additional services is another powerful verbal communication tool. It shows your understanding customer needs and your commitment to providing value. As Peter Drucker aptly put it,

*"The aim of marketing is to know and understand
the customer so well the product or service
fits him and sells itself."*

In the depths of my memory, I recall a time when my consultations were far from professional. I cringe as I remember how I used to stand above my clients, nonchalantly flipping through folders and allowing my attention to wander. There was a time when I failed to listen and connect with those seeking my guidance.

However, I think those times have become stories that I can laugh at and consider past my transformative power of attentiveness and its profound impact on my consultations.

Often, I would stand above my clients, towering over them with an air of indifference. I would casually fold my arms, and my eyes would dart around the room as if searching for something more interesting than the person before me. Sometimes, I would even succumb to the temptation of checking my phone, oblivious to the message it sent to my guests - that they were not worthy of my undivided attention.

One day, a client approached me with a heavy heart, seeking solace and guidance. As they poured their heart out, I realized the gravity of my actions. I had made them feel unheard and insignificant. It was a wake-up call that shook me to my core. I knew I had to make a change. Determined to improve, I embarked on a journey of self-reflection and growth. I recognized that active listening was the key to building trust and establishing a genuine connection with my clients. I decided to sit at eye level with them, creating an environment of equality and respect. This simple shift in physical positioning conveyed that I valued their presence and was ready to listen.

To be honest, my mind was wandering when that guest told me her father just passed away. I just replied something unknowingly. Great! Once again, oops!

To demonstrate my attentiveness, I began repeating what I thought I understood from their words. This not only ensured that I comprehended their message accurately but also made them feel heard and validated. I learned to set aside distractions, leaving my phone in my office or locker to give my undivided attention to those who sought my guidance.

I witnessed a remarkable transformation in my consultations as I implemented these changes. Clients began to open up more freely, knowing they had my full attention and support.

They felt valued and understood, fostering a deeper connection and trust. The results were astounding - better outcomes, increased client satisfaction, and a stronger sense of fulfillment in my work.

Looking back on my journey, I am grateful for the realization that attentiveness is a powerful tool in building meaningful connections. By making minor shifts in the attention I gave my clients, I was able to create a safe space for them to share their thoughts and concerns. I learned that true listening requires hearing words, understanding the emotions and intentions behind them, and repeating what I understood they were saying.

This story serves as a reminder that small changes can have a profound impact on our interactions with others. By practicing active listening, sitting at eye level, and eliminating distractions, we can forge deeper connections, foster trust, and achieve better results. Let us remember the power of attentiveness and its transformative effect on our consultations and relationships.

'*Buy words*' are another potent tool in verbal communication. These words or phrases trigger a positive psychological response, encouraging the listener to take action. Examples of '*Buy Words'* include '*exclusive*,' '*limited time offer*,' '*guaranteed*,' '*proven*,' and '*value*.' These words create a sense of urgency, exclusivity, and trust, making the listener more likely to make a purchase. As Maya Angelou once said,

"Words mean more than what is set down on paper. It takes the human voice to infuse them with deeper meaning."

Non-verbal communication is equally important. When interacting with guests, accompanying them to different areas and pointing out products or displays can create a more personalized and engaging experience. As Amy Cuddy states,

"Body language shapes who you are."

Body language is a significant part of non-verbal communication. It can show interest or disinterest, even without saying a word. For example, maintaining eye contact and leaning in shows you are engaged and interested while crossing your arms and looking away can signal disinterest or discomfort.

Expressing a positive attitude through both verbal and non-verbal cues is crucial. A smile, a friendly tone of voice, and positive words can make the listener feel valued and appreciated. Remember, it is not just your body that speaks without words but also your surroundings. Is your store and bathroom clean? How does your store's front look? Is your parking lot clean and garbage cans emptied? How do you look physically? Do you look awake? Is your hair groomed? Are your clothes clean? Or do you look hungover from yesterday's clothes?

These are just a few examples. Remember, how you look shows you care and also displays your confidence.

"People may hear your words, but they feel your attitude."
                                                    - John C. Maxwell

This quote conveys the idea that your attitude, whether expressed through words or non-verbal cues, plays a significant role in how others perceive you and can ultimately impact your success and relationships.

In conclusion, both verbal and non-verbal communication play a significant role in the power of consultation. By mastering these skills, you can effectively engage with your audience in person or on social media and drive positive outcomes. As George Bernard Shaw famously said,

"The single biggest problem in communication is the illusion that it has taken place."

Therefore, ensure your communication is clear, effective, and meaningful.

Exercise 1: Practice Active Listening. Active listening is a crucial part of effective communication. Spend a day consciously focusing on listening more than you speak. Whether you're interacting with a colleague, a friend, or a family member, try to fully understand their perspective before responding.

Exercise 2: Experiment with 'Buy Words.' Create a social media post for a product or service using 'Buy Words.' Monitor the engagement on this post compared to others and note any differences you observe.

Exercise 3: Role-Play Customer Interaction. With a partner, role-play a customer interaction scenario. One person is the customer, and the other is the consultant—practice using both verbal and non-verbal communication skills to create a positive customer experience.

Exercise 4: Body Language Awareness. Spend a day being mindful of your body language. Notice how you sit, stand, and move when you're interacting with others. Are you conveying openness and interest? Or could your body language be interpreted as closed off or disinterested?

Exercise 5: Positive Attitude Expression. For a week, make a conscious effort to express a positive attitude through your words and actions. Notice how this impacts your interactions with others.

Exercise 6: Feedback and Improvement. Ask for feedback from colleagues or friends about your communication skills. What do they think you do well? What could you improve? Use this feedback to identify areas for improvement and make a plan to work on these areas.

Practice these exercises regularly to enhance your communication skills and become a more effective consultant. One last thing: Take a good look in the mirror and ask yourself: *What am I saying about myself*? Do this without opening your mouth.

CHAPTER 4

BANDING YOURSELF ON SOCIAL MEDIA

anding yourself on social media involves carefully managing your online presence and communication skills to create a positive and professional image. Both verbal and non-verbal skills play a crucial role in shaping how others perceive you online. Here are some do's and don'ts to consider:

Verbal Skills (Written Communication):

Do:

1. **Be mindful of your tone**: Use a polite and respectful tone in your written communication. Avoid sarcasm, aggression, or offensive language that others may misinterpret.

2. **Use proper grammar and spelling**: Ensure your posts and comments are well-written and free of grammatical errors. Proofread your content before sharing it to maintain professionalism.

3. **Engage in meaningful conversations**: Contribute to conversations in a constructive manner. Share your insights,

ask thoughtful questions, and respond respectfully to others' opinions.

4. **Be authentic and genuine**: Honestly share your thoughts, experiences, and expertise. People appreciate authenticity and can easily identify when someone is being insincere.

Don't:

1. Engage in online arguments or trolling: Avoid getting involved in heated debates or confrontations. Engaging in hostile exchanges can harm your online reputation and damage relationships.

2. Share inappropriate or offensive content: Refrain from posting or sharing is offensive, discriminatory, or disrespectful content. Such content can have severe consequences and tarnish your personal or professional image.

3. Overusing jargon or slang: While using some industry-specific jargon or slang is acceptable, it can confuse or alienate your audience. Aim for clear and concise communication that everyone easily understands.

4. Neglect proofreading: Always proofread your posts and comments before sharing them. Typos and grammatical errors can make you appear careless and unprofessional.

Non-Verbal Skills (Visual Communication):

Do:

1. **Use professional profile pictures**: Choose a profile picture that presents you in a professional and approachable manner. Avoid using inappropriate or overly casual images that may give a negative impression.
2. **Share high-quality images and videos**: When sharing visual content, ensure it is of high quality and relevant to your message. Clear and visually appealing media can enhance your credibility.
3. **Maintain consistency in branding**: If you're promoting a personal brand or business, use consistent colors, fonts, and visual elements across your social media profiles. This helps create a cohesive and recognizable image.
4. **Show empathy and emotional intelligence**: Non-verbal cues such as emojis can be used to convey emotions and empathy in your online interactions. However, use them sparingly and appropriately to avoid misinterpretation.

Don't:

1. **Post inappropriate or offensive images**: Avoid sharing provocative or inappropriate images. Remember that once something is online, it can be challenging to remove it entirely.
2. **Overshare personal information**: Be cautious about sharing personal details such as your address, phone number, or financial information. Protect your privacy and minimize the risk of identity theft or fraud.
3. **Display aggressive or negative body language**: Even though social media is primarily text-based, your non-verbal skills still

matter. Avoid using excessive capitalization, multiple exclamation marks, or aggressive language, as they can be perceived as argumentative or rude.

4. **Neglect your profile to update it regularly**: Keep your profile information up to date, including your job title, contact information, and any relevant achievements. Outdated or inaccurate information can create confusion and diminish your credibility.

Consistency is key in branding and is crucial for building a strong and recognizable brand identity. It's essential to start with a clear and well-defined brand strategy to stay consistent with your branding. This includes establishing brand guidelines that encompass your brand's visual elements, such as logo, colors, typography, and imagery, as well as your brand's tone of voice and messaging.

Consistency should be maintained across all touchpoints, from your website and social media profiles to marketing materials and customer interactions. Regularly review and update your brand guidelines as needed to ensure they remain relevant and aligned with your evolving business goals. Additionally, empower your team to understand and implement these guidelines consistently. By adhering to a cohesive brand strategy, you can reinforce brand recognition, build trust with your audience, and create a lasting, memorable impression in the minds of your customers.

CHAPTER 5

HOW TO USE THE CAMERA FOR SM

U sing the camera effectively on social media can be a powerful way to engage viewers and create a lasting impact. Here are some tips on how to engage the viewer using both verbal and nonverbal skills:

When I first started using the camera, I was all over the place with my body moments and eye contact. I would often turn my back to the camera as if I were speaking to the wall.

The other challenge was that the camera didn't respond as a live audience would, and I felt like I was talking to an empty room. I was used to feeding off the audience or maybe getting a laugh from one of my jokes. Initially, I would just freeze and lose my thoughts because I only saw a little black camera hole. Now I just picture an audience from my live events as infants. The good news is the more you practice, the easier it gets when it's just you and the camera.

Here are some tips to help you when you start creating your videos.

Verbal Skills:

1. Captions that tell a story: Tell a story or ask questions when posting photos or videos. Use captions that provide context. This encourages viewers to engage with your content and start conversations.

2. Authentic and relatable narratives: Share personal experiences, anecdotes, or behind-the-scenes stories related to the visual content. Authenticity and relatability can create a stronger connection with your audience.

3. Encourage interaction: Prompt your viewers to engage with your content by asking for their opinions, thoughts, or experiences. This can be done through captions or by verbally expressing a question or call to action in videos.

4. Communicate your message clearly: If your visual content aims to convey a specific message or promote a cause, use the camera to support your verbal explanation. Clearly articulate your message, providing context and information that enhances the viewer's understanding.

Nonverbal Skills:

1. **Visual composition**: Pay attention to the composition of your photos or videos. Utilize techniques such as the rule of thirds, leading lines, or symmetry to create visually appealing and engaging content.

2. **Expressive body language**: In videos or live streams, use expressive body language to convey enthusiasm, confidence, or any other desired emotion. Your nonverbal cues can enhance the impact of your message and captivate your viewers.

3. **Eye contact**: Maintain eye contact with the camera lens when filming videos or taking selfies. This creates a sense of connection as if you are directly engaging with your viewers.

4. **Use gestures and facial expressions**: Utilize gestures and facial expressions to emphasize and convey emotions. This can make your content more dynamic and engaging, as viewers feel more connected to your message.

5. **Visual storytelling**: Leverage the camera to tell stories visually. Use techniques such as close-ups, wide shots, or creative angles to evoke emotions, build suspense, or highlight important details.

Remember, both verbal and nonverbal skills work in tandem to engage the viewer. By combining compelling narratives, clear communication, and visually captivating content, you can create a powerful impact on social media and forge deeper connections with your audience.

CHAPTER 6

THE POWER OF SOCIAL MEDIA:

AMPLIFYING BRANDING AND
CONNECTING WITH YOUR
TARGET AUDIENCE

In today's digital age, social media has become a powerful tool for communication and connection. It has revolutionized how we interact, share information, and build relationships. This chapter explores the stories of great speakers who have harnessed the power of social media to effectively communicate their branding and sell their services to their target audience. We will delve into their strategies, the impact of their online presence, and the lessons we can learn from their success.

One of the greatest things that inspired me was studying many great influencers or shopping networks.

Section 1: Leveraging Social Media for Branding

Social media platforms offer a unique opportunity to showcase your brand and establish yourself as an authority in your field. Great speakers understand the importance of consistent branding across their social media profiles. They carefully curate their content, ensuring it aligns with their expertise and resonates with their target audience. By leveraging social media, they create a cohesive and recognizable brand that attracts and engages followers.

Section 2: Building an Engaged Community

Successful speakers recognize that social media is just about broadcasting their message and building a community. They actively engage with their audience by responding to comments, initiating conversations, and providing valuable insights.

By fostering a sense of community, they create a loyal following that not only supports their brand but also becomes advocates for their services.

Section 3: Authenticity and Transparency

Authenticity is key to establishing trust and credibility on social media. Great speakers understand the importance of being genuine and transparent in their online presence. They share personal stories, lessons learned, and behind-the-scenes glimpses into their lives. By being authentic, they connect with their audience deeper, fostering a sense of relatability and building lasting relationships.

Section 4: Creating Compelling Content

Content is the currency of social media. Great speakers know how to create compelling content that captivates their audience and drives engagement. They share valuable insights, thought-provoking ideas, and actionable tips. They utilize various formats such as videos, blog posts, infographics, and live streams to cater to different preferences.

By consistently delivering high-quality content, they position themselves as trusted authorities and attract their target audience.

Section 5: Leveraging Influencer Collaborations

Collaborating with influencers in their niche is another strategy great speakers employ to expand their reach and connect with a broader audience. By partnering with influencers who share similar values and target the same audience, they tap into established communities and gain exposure to new followers. These collaborations help them amplify their branding and increase their chances of selling their services to a larger audience.

Conclusion:

Social media has transformed how speakers communicate and connect with their target audience. By leveraging social media platforms effectively, great speakers have been able to amplify their branding, build engaged communities, and sell their services to a broader audience.

Their success lies in curating consistent branding, fostering authenticity, creating compelling content, and leveraging influencer collaborations. As we navigate the world of social media, let us learn from these great speakers and harness the power of social media to communicate our branding and connect with our target audience, ultimately driving the success of our speaking ventures.

Some great influencers that use social media powerfully and effectively:

In the digital age, many great speakers have harnessed the power of social media to communicate their brand, connect with their audience, and sell their services. Now, we will look into the profiles of some of these influential speakers, their strategies, and the platforms they use to disseminate their wisdom and knowledge.

The Social Media Maestros: Great Speakers and Their Platforms:

Gary Vaynerchuk

Gary Vaynerchuk, also known as Gary Vee, is a renowned entrepreneur, author, and speaker. He has effectively used social media platforms like Instagram, Twitter, and LinkedIn to share his insights on entrepreneurship and digital marketing. His energetic and straightforward style has resonated with millions. His books, including *"Crush It!"* and *"Jab, Jab, Jab, Right Hook,"* are excellent resources for understanding the power of social media. His website, garyvaynerchuk.com, is a treasure trove of articles, videos, and podcasts.

Brene Brown

Brene Brown, a research professor and best-selling author, has used social media to share her insights on vulnerability, courage, and empathy. Her TED talks have gone viral, and her engaging posts on Instagram and Twitter have garnered a large following. Her books, such as *"Daring Greatly"* and *"The Gifts of Imperfection,"* offer deep insights into her research. Her website, brenebrown.com, provides access to her blog, podcast, and online learning opportunities.

Simon Sinek

A motivational speaker and author, Simon Sinek, has used social media to spread his ideas about leadership and finding one's *"why."* His TED talk, *"Start with Why,"* is one of the most viewed videos of all time. He regularly shares thought-provoking content on LinkedIn, Twitter, and Instagram. His books, including *"Start with Why"* and *"Leaders Eat Last,"* delve deeper into his philosophies. His website, simonsinek.com, offers access to his blog, podcast, and online classes.

Mel Robbins

Mel Robbins, a motivational speaker, author, and television host, has used social media to share her practical, science-backed advice for overcoming procrastination and improving productivity. Her *"5 Second Rule"* has gained widespread popularity on platforms like Instagram, YouTube, and Twitter. Her book, *"The 5 Second Rule,"* provides a comprehensive understanding of her technique. Her website, melrobbins.com, offers a wealth of resources, including articles, videos, and online courses.

Conclusion:

These great speakers have effectively used social media to communicate their branding, connect with their target audience, and sell their services. They have leveraged their online presence to share their wisdom and knowledge, inspiring millions worldwide. We can gather invaluable insights and learn from their success by exploring their books, websites, and social media platforms. As we navigate our own journeys, let us harness the power of social media to amplify our voices, share our wisdom, and connect with our audience.

CHAPTER 7

THE SERVICE AREA AND EXPERIENCE

Title 1: Enhancing Guest Experience: Effective Strategies for In-Person and Social Media Interactions

Excellent customer service is the number one job
in any company!
It is the personality of the company and the reason customers come
back.
Without customers, there is no company!

- Connie Elder

Trust me when I say this: *Maintaining a high level of integrity in sales is paramount.* There's a substantial 90% chance of repeat business when a customer buys from you, and this statistic underscores the importance of ethical sales practices. Sadly, some salespeople may resort to overselling products that customers don't genuinely require, driven by greed and dishonesty. However, those with true integrity and a genuine concern for their customers understand that the path to long-term success lies in acting in the customer's best interest. This includes providing them with the information and products they genuinely need and educating them about potential upgrades or enhancements that can enhance their experience.

This guidance can be valuable in a world where technology and products are continually evolving. Building trust is the key to fostering repeat business because customers rely on us to offer genuine solutions and avoid the pitfalls of overselling. People can often discern when they are being misled, and ethical sales professionals strive to be known for their honesty and customer-first approach. After all, who wants to be known for anything less?

Providing an exceptional guest experience is paramount, whether it's in-person or social media.

Here are some strategies to serve your guests more effectively and ensure they have a memorable experience:

1. **Verbal Serving**: Communication is vital in any interaction. Use clear, concise, and respectful language when speaking to your guests. Be attentive to their needs and respond promptly. While you're face to face, maintain eye contact and use a friendly tone. Use a professional yet approachable tone on social media, and ensure your responses are timely and helpful.

2. **Asking Comforting Questions**: Show genuine interest in your guests by asking questions that make them feel comfortable and valued. These could be about their day, preferences, or feedback about your service. This helps build rapport and provides valuable insights into how you can serve them better.

3. **Providing Positive Feedback**: When guests express negative feelings or dissatisfaction, respond with empathy and positivity. Acknowledge their feelings, apologize if necessary,

and offer solutions. This approach shows that you value their feedback and are committed to improving their experience.

4. **Demonstrating Processes**: Whether you're explaining a process in person or posting a tutorial on social media, ensure your instructions are clear and easy to follow. Step-by-step show them how you're doing it and how they can replicate it. This not only educates your guests but also builds their confidence in your expertise.

5. **Creating a Relaxing Environment**: Make your guests feel relaxed and comfortable. In-person, this could mean maintaining a clean and welcoming space, offering a warm greeting, or providing a comforting ambiance with soft music or pleasant scents. On social media, maintain a positive and engaging online presence. Share uplifting content, respond to comments and messages in a friendly manner, and create a community where your guests feel valued and heard.

By implementing these strategies, you can enhance your guests' experience and ensure they leave with a positive impression.

Remember, the goal is to meet their expectations and exceed them. By doing so, you'll create loyal guests and advocates who will recommend your service to others online or in person.

Title 2: Nonverbal Communication: Enhancing Guest Experience through Professionalism and Preparedness

Nonverbal communication plays a crucial role in providing an exceptional guest experience. It's not just about what we say but also about how we present ourselves and our environment. Here are some strategies to enhance your nonverbal communication skills and serve your guests more effectively.

1. **Using the Right Equipment, Supplies, and Tools:** The tools you use in your service speak volumes about your professionalism. Ensure they are clean, well-maintained, and of high quality. This enhances your service delivery and shows your guests that you value quality and hygiene.

2. **Maintaining a Clean and Organized Environment**: A clean and organized environment is a nonverbal indicator of professionalism. Take the time to tidy up your workspace, arrange your tools neatly, and ensure your environment is welcoming and comfortable for your guests.

3. **Demonstrating Professionalism**: Nonverbal cues such as your attire, posture, and demeanor can significantly impact your guests' perception of your professionalism. Dress appropriately, maintain good posture, and exhibit a positive and confident demeanor.

4. **Explaining Key Points and Target Goals**: Use visual aids or demonstrations to illustrate critical points or target goals. This can help your guests understand your process better and set clear expectations.

5. **Recommending Services:** When recommending services, use brochures, samples, or demonstrations. This gives your guests a tangible understanding of what they can expect.

6. **Practicing Service Delivery**: Practice makes perfect. Conduct role-plays or use mirror exercises to practice your service delivery. This can help you identify areas for improvement and enhance your nonverbal communication skills.

Remember, *"Excellence is not a skill, it's an attitude."*- Ralph Marston. By incorporating these strategies, you can convey your professionalism non-verbally and provide an exceptional guest experience.

The main point of all these strategies is to emphasize the importance of nonverbal communication in creating a positive guest experience. Just as in the story you mentioned, when we visit a restaurant, we have certain expectations.

We want to be seated at a clean table, provided with clean silverware, and served food that is timely and presented well. We expect a level of professionalism from the staff, including cleanliness and attentiveness.

By focusing on nonverbal cues such as cleanliness, organization, and professionalism, we can exceed these expectations and create a memorable experience for our guests. Nonverbal communication sets the tone for the entire interaction, conveying our commitment to quality, attention to detail, and respect for our guests.

Consider this scenario: *You've shared enticing images and descriptions of your restaurant's pristine ambiance and delectable food offerings on social media. People are eagerly drawn to your establishment, expecting to encounter the exceptional experience you portrayed online. However, when they arrive at your restaurant, do their expectations align with the reality they encounter?*

By incorporating the strategies mentioned earlier, such as using clean and well-maintained equipment, maintaining a clean and organized environment, and demonstrating professionalism, we can ensure that our guests feel respected, comfortable, and confident in our services.

Ultimately, the main idea is that nonverbal communication is a powerful tool in creating a positive guest experience. It goes beyond words and speaks volumes about our professionalism, attention to detail, and commitment to exceeding expectations. By paying attention to these nonverbal cues, we can leave a lasting impression on our guests and build strong relationships based on trust and satisfaction.

CHAPTER 8

RETAIL AREA:

THE POWER OF VERBAL AND NON-VERBAL COMMUNICATION IN RETAIL SETUPS

The retail setup of a business is a silent communicator that speaks volumes about the brand. It's not just about the products you sell but how you present them. This chapter explores the power of verbal and non-verbal communication in creating a well-stocked, clean, and inviting retail area. We will delve into the importance of maintaining a beautiful retail space through insightful quotes and practical exercises.

Section 1: The Power of Verbal Communication

1. "The way you describe your products can make them come alive in the customer's mind."

- Unknown

This quote emphasizes the power of effective product descriptions. It highlights that by using compelling and vivid language, businesses can create a solid mental image of their products in customers minds. When done well, this can significantly enhance the appeal of the products and drive sales.

2. "A well-informed salesperson is a walking, talking advertisement for your brand."

- Unknown

This quote underscores the importance of knowledgeable and informed salespeople in representing a brand. When salespeople possess in-depth knowledge about the products or services they are selling, they become living embodiments of the brand's expertise and credibility, instilling customer confidence.

3. "Your words can paint a picture of abundance and quality, making customers feel they are in a well-stocked store."

- Unknown

This quote highlights the influence of language in creating an inviting shopping experience. Through effective communication, businesses can convey the impression of a store filled with high-quality products, enticing customers and making them feel they are in the right place to find what they need.

Exercise: Practice describing your products in a way that highlights their features and benefits. Use positive, engaging language that makes customers want to learn more.

Section 2: The Power of Non-Verbal Communication

1. "A clean, well-organized store is a silent ambassador of your brand."

- Unknown

This quote underscores the significance of the physical environment in shaping a brand's image. An impeccably clean and thoughtfully organized store communicates professionalism, attention to detail, and a commitment to excellence, all of which silently endorse the brand's reputation.

2. "The visual appeal of your store is a non-verbal invitation for customers to explore."

- Unknown

This quote emphasizes the power of aesthetics in attracting and engaging customers. The way a store looks, from its storefront to its interior design, conveys an unspoken invitation for customers to step inside, explore its offerings, and experience what the brand offer.

3. "A well-stocked store communicates abundance and reliability to customers."

-Unknown

This quote highlights the importance of maintaining sufficient inventory. When customers see a store filled with products and options, it conveys reliability and the assurance that their needs will be met. It creates a sense of abundance, making them more likely to trust and shop at the store.

"4. The layout of your store can guide customers on a journey, leading them to discover and purchase more."

- Unknown

This quote suggests that the store's layout is a strategic tool for influencing customer behavior. A well-designed layout can lead customers on a planned journey through the store, making it more likely that they will discover and purchase additional items. It showcases the importance of thoughtful store design in boosting sales and customer satisfaction.

Exercise: Regularly review your store layout. Is it easy to navigate? Are your products displayed in a way that is appealing and makes sense? Make necessary adjustments to enhance the shopping experience.

Section 3: Maintaining a Beautiful Retail Space

1. "Keeping your store clean and well-stocked is an ongoing commitment to your customers."

- Unknown

This quote underscores the importance of maintaining a high standard of cleanliness and ensuring products are readily available to customers. It highlights that these efforts are not one-time tasks but an ongoing commitment to consistently meeting customers' needs and expectations.

2. "An inviting retail space is like a welcoming home - it makes customers feel comfortable and eager to return."

- Unknown

This quote draws a parallel between a comfortable, inviting home and a welcoming retail environment. It emphasizes that a store's ambiance, layout, and atmosphere play a vital role in making customers feel at ease and valued. Such an environment encourages repeat visits and customer loyalty.

3. "Every detail in your store- from lighting to signage, contributes to the overall shopping experience."

- Unknown

This quote emphasizes the holistic nature of the shopping experience. It suggests that even minor details, such as lighting and signage, play a crucial role in shaping how customers perceive and interact with the store. Attention to these details can enhance the overall shopping experience and leave a lasting impression on customers.

Exercise: Create a cleaning and restocking schedule to ensure your store looks its best. Regularly walk through your store as if you were a customer and note any areas that need improvement.

Section 4: The Integration of Verbal and Non-Verbal Communication

1. "When your verbal communication aligns with your retail setup, it creates a cohesive and engaging shopping experience."

- Unknown

This quote underscores the importance of consistency in retail. Effective communication isn't just about spoken words but also about ensuring that what is said matches the overall in-store experience. When there's alignment between verbal communication and the retail environment, it fosters a seamless and captivating shopping experience.

2. "The power of communication in retail lies in the harmony between what you say and what customers see and feel in your store."

- Unknown

This quote emphasizes that communication in retail isn't limited to words alone. It recognizes that the most potent form of communication occurs when what is said aligns with the visual and emotional aspects of the in-store experience. This harmony between words, visuals, and emotions is what truly resonates with customers and drives engagement.

Exercise: Train your staff to communicate effectively about your products and brand. Their verbal communication should complement the visual appeal of your store.

Conclusion:

The power of verbal and non-verbal communication extends beyond personal interactions to the very setup of your retail space. A well-stocked, clean, and inviting store communicates a commitment to quality and customer satisfaction.

By maintaining a beautiful retail area and aligning it with effective verbal communication, businesses can create a memorable shopping experience that keeps customers coming back. As retailers, let's harness the power of communication to create retail spaces, sell products, and tell our brand story.

Adapting the principles of verbal and non-verbal communication to the realm of social media selling requires a thoughtful approach. While the physical retail setup may not be applicable, the following suggestions can help create a similar impact in the digital space:

The Power of Verbal Communication:

- **Craft compelling product descriptions**: Use engaging language that vividly describes your product's features, benefits, and unique selling points.
- **Develop a consistent brand voice**: Establish a distinct tone and style in your written content that aligns with your brand identity and resonates with your target audience.
- **Respond promptly and courteously**: When engaging with customers through comments or direct messages, ensure your responses are timely, helpful, and friendly.

The Power of Non-Verbal Communication:

- **Visual appeal through imagery**: Use high-quality product photos and graphics to showcase your products.
- **Consistent branding**: Maintain a cohesive visual identity across your social media profiles, including color schemes, fonts, and logo placement.

- **Create a sense of abundance**: Regularly update your social media feeds with new product releases, restocks, or limited-time offers to convey a sense of availability and variety.

Maintaining a Beautiful Digital Space:

- **Regular content curation**: Keep your social media profiles organized and clutter-free by regularly reviewing and removing outdated or irrelevant posts.
- **Optimize user experience**: Ensure your website or online store is user-friendly, easy to navigate, and visually appealing to enhance the overall digital shopping experience.
- **Pay attention to details**: From well-designed cover photos to consistent image sizing, focus on the small details that contribute to a polished and professional online presence.

The Integration of Verbal and Non-Verbal Communication:

- **Consistency in messaging**: Ensure that the language used in your captions, comments, and direct messages aligns with your brand voice and values.
- **Visual storytelling**: Utilize social media features like Instagram Stories or Facebook Live to showcase behind-the-scenes content, product demonstrations, or customer testimonials.
- **Engage with your audience**: Actively respond to comments, messages, and reviews to foster a sense of connection and build customer trust.

Conclusion:

While the retail setup may differ in the context of social media selling, the principles of verbal and non-verbal communication remain crucial. Businesses can create a similar impact online by effectively utilizing verbal communication through compelling descriptions, consistent brand messaging, and leveraging non-verbal communication through visually appealing imagery and a well-curated digital space.

Remember! Maintaining a beautiful digital presence requires attention to detail, consistency, and active engagement with your audience.

CHAPTER 9

THE POWER OF VERBAL AND NON-VERBAL ACTIONS IN CLOSING A SALE

"Closing the deal is not just the end of a transaction; it's the beginning of a long-lasting relationship."

\- Zig Ziglar

Zig Ziglar, a renowned motivational speaker, and sales expert, emphasizes the significance of closing the deal as the start of a lasting relationship. Just as a strong greeting sets the tone for a successful interaction, closing a deal is equally important. This section explores why closing is crucial, highlighting the importance of consistency throughout the sales process. This will be easy if we are honest and consistent from beginning to end.

The Importance of Closing and Consistency

Zig Ziglar's quote encapsulates the essence of why closing the deal is as vital as the initial greeting. Here are a few reasons why:

1. **Solidifies Commitment**: Closing the deal signifies the customer has committed to purchase. It solidifies their decision and establishes a sense of trust and reliability in the salesperson and the product or service they're offering.

2. **Achieves Desired Outcome**: The closing stage is where the salesperson's efforts culminate in achieving the desired outcome - a successful sale. It is the ultimate goal of the sales process and a crucial step toward meeting business objectives.

3. **Builds Customer Relationships**: Closing the deal is not the end; it marks the beginning of a long-term relationship with the customer. By ensuring a smooth and positive closing experience, sales professionals lay the foundation for future interactions, repeat business, and potential referrals.

Consistency is vital throughout the sales process, including the greeting and closing stages. Here's why consistency is crucial:

1. **Establishes Trust**: Consistency in communication, behavior, and service delivery builds customer trust. When sales professionals consistently deliver on their promises and maintain a consistent approach, customers feel confident purchasing.

2. **Reinforces Brand Identity**: Consistency in messaging, branding, and customer experience enhances the brand identity. It creates a cohesive and recognizable image, making it easier for customers to connect with and remember the brand.

3. **Enhances Customer Experience**: Consistency in the sales process ensures a seamless and positive customer experience. From the initial greeting to the closing, maintaining consistency in interactions, product information, and service quality helps customers feel valued and satisfied.

Conclusion:

Closing the deal is not just the end of a transaction; it marks the beginning of a lasting relationship with the customer. Just as a strong greeting sets the stage for a successful interaction, the closing is equally vital in achieving the desired outcome and building trust.

Consistency throughout the sales process- from the greeting to the closing, reinforces trust, establishes brand identity, and enhances the overall customer experience. By understanding the significance of both closing and consistency, sales professionals can foster long-term relationships and drive business success.

Closing a sale is critical in sales, where effective verbal and non-verbal actions can make all the difference. Whether in-person interaction or an online sale through social media, understanding how to communicate and engage with customers is vital. This chapter explores the power of verbal and non-verbal actions in successfully closing a sale, providing insightful quotes and practical exercises to enhance your closing techniques.

Section 1: Verbal Actions for In-Person Sales Closing

❖ *The right words at the right time can seal the deal and turn a potential customer into a satisfied and lifelong buyer.*

❖ *Confidence in your product and persuasive language can instill trust and compel customers to purchase.*

❖ *Active listening and effective questioning can uncover customer needs and provide tailored solutions, leading to a successful close.*

Practice role-playing scenarios where you engage with potential customers, focusing on using persuasive language, active listening, and asking relevant questions to guide them toward a purchase decision.

Section 2: Non-Verbal Actions for In-Person Sales Closing

Your body language speaks volumes - stand tall, maintain eye contact, and exude confidence to inspire trust that your customers have made the right decision.

A warm smile and a firm handshake can create a positive and memorable impression, enhancing the likelihood of a successful close.

Gestures and facial expressions that convey enthusiasm and excitement about your product can influence customers' emotions and increase their desire to close the deal.

Practice your non-verbal communication skills by recording yourself during mock sales interactions. Pay attention to your posture, facial expressions, and gestures, adjusting to project confidence and approachability.

Section 3: Verbal Actions for Online Sales Closing through Social Media

❖ *Craft compelling and concise product descriptions that highlight the value and benefits, capturing the attention of potential customers.*

❖ *Engage with customers through personalized messages, responding promptly to inquiries, and providing additional information to facilitate the final decision-making.*

❖ *Utilize persuasive language and call-to-action statements in your social media posts to encourage customers to take the final step toward purchasing.*

Create sample social media posts or messages that effectively communicate the value of your products, incorporating persuasive language and clear calls to action. Seek feedback from peers or mentors to refine your approach.

Section 4: Non-Verbal Actions for Online Sales Closing through Social Media

❖ *Visual appeal is crucial in online sales - use high-quality product images, videos, and graphics to capture attention and create a desire to buy.*

❖ *Consistent branding across your social media profiles and website fosters trust and recognition, enhancing the likelihood of closing a sale.*

❖ *Prompt and professional responses to comments, reviews, and direct messages demonstrate your commitment to customer satisfaction and building trust and loyalty to others.*

Conduct an audit of your social media profiles and website, ensuring consistent branding, high-quality visuals, and timely responses to customer interactions. Make necessary adjustments to enhance the overall online shopping experience.

Conclusion:

Closing a sale requires a combination of effective verbal and non-verbal actions, whether it's in-person or online through social media. You can guide customers toward a purchase decision by mastering persuasive language, active listening, and tailored solutions. Additionally, projecting confidence, approachability, and enthusiasm through non-verbal cues can significantly impact customer perception. In the online realm, compelling product descriptions, engaging messages, and visually appealing content play a crucial role in closing a sale. Remember, practice and refinement of verbal and non-verbal actions are key to becoming a skilled sales closer.

CHAPTER 10

THE ART OF FOLLOWING UP:

MAINTAINING CONNECTION AND DRIVING FURTHER SALES

"Every contact we have with a customer influences whether or not they'll come back. We have to be great every time, or we'll lose them."

- Kevin Stirtz

K evin Stirtz, a renowned author and customer service expert, emphasizes the importance of every interaction with a customer, including the follow-up after a sale. This chapter explores the power of verbal and non-verbal actions in maintaining connections and driving further sales, providing practical examples and suggestions for effective follow-up strategies.

I found that keeping a true relationship with your guest will keep them coming back, as they want to support you as much as you have supported them. Not just by calling them to keep selling because there is a sale but to know their Birthdays or holiday greetings or a blue call or email, text message asking about how they are, how their family is doing, and how they are still enjoying what they bought. This takes a short time to do but will impact and strengthen the relationship.

Section 1: Verbal Follow-Up Strategies for In-Person Sales

1. **Personalized Thank You Notes**: A handwritten thank you note is a powerful verbal tool that shows appreciation and personal attention. It can include a message expressing gratitude for their purchase and an invitation for future interactions.
2. **Phone Calls**: A follow-up phone call lets you verbally express your appreciation, answer any questions, and suggest additional products or services. It's a personal touch that can strengthen the customer relationship.
3. **Customer Surveys**: Surveys allow customers to express their satisfaction and provide feedback. This verbal interaction can provide valuable insights for improving your products or services.

Exercise:

- Practice writing personalized thank-you notes and conducting follow-up phone calls.
- Develop a customer survey that can help you gather feedback and improve your offerings.

Section 2: Non-Verbal Follow-Up Strategies for In-Person Sales

1. **Gifts or Tokens of Appreciation**: Small gifts or tokens can serve as a non-verbal thank you, reinforcing your appreciation and keeping your business in mind.
2. **Loyalty Programs**: Loyalty programs, such as points or rewards systems, are a non-verbal way of encouraging repeat business and maintaining a connection with customers.
3. **Product Demonstrations or Workshops**: Inviting customers to product demonstrations or workshops can provide a hands-on experience and deepen their connection with your products or services.

Exercise:

- Consider what types of gifts or tokens could be appropriate for your business.
- Develop a loyalty program that encourages repeat business.
- Plan a product demonstration or workshop that can engage your customers.

Section 3: Verbal Follow-Up Strategies for Online Sales through Social Media

1. **Follow-Up Emails**: A personalized follow-up email can express gratitude, provide additional product information, and invite future interactions.
2. **Social Media Engagement**: Engaging with customers on social media through comments, likes, and shares can maintain the connection and encourage further sales.
3. **Webinars or Live Q&A Sessions**: Hosting webinars or live Q&A sessions can provide valuable information, answer customer questions, and promote your products or services.

Exercise:

- Draft a follow-up email that can be personalized for each customer.
- Plan a social media strategy that encourages engagement.
- Consider hosting a webinar or live Q&A session to connect with your customers.

Section 4: Non-Verbal Follow-Up Strategies
for Online Sales through Social Media

1. **Retargeting Ads**: Retargeting ads can remind customers of your products or services, encouraging repeat business.
2. **Personalized Recommendations**: You can provide personalized product recommendations based on their purchase history, enhancing their shopping experience.
3. **Regular Social Media Updates**: Regular updates about new products, promotions, or company news can keep your customers engaged and informed.

Exercise:

- Develop a retargeting ad campaign.
- Consider how you can provide personalized recommendations to your customers.
- Plan regular social media updates to keep your customers engaged.

Conclusion:

Following up with customers after a sale is crucial in maintaining connections and driving further sales. Whether through verbal actions like personalized thank-you notes and follow-up phone calls or non-verbal actions like gifts and loyalty programs, these strategies can enhance customer relationships and encourage repeat business.

In the online realm, follow-up emails, social media engagement, and regular updates can keep customers engaged and informed. By mastering the art of following up, you can foster long-term relationships and drive business success.

A strong follow-up with customers is crucial for future sales in both brick-and-mortar businesses and online sales. Here are a few reasons why it is so important:

1. **Customer Retention**: Following up with customers demonstrates that you value their business and care about their satisfaction. It helps build a strong relationship and fosters loyalty, increasing the likelihood of repeat purchases and long-term customer retention.

2. **Upselling and Cross-selling Opportunities**: A follow-up provides an opportunity to suggest complementary products or services that align with the customer's previous purchase. By understanding their needs and preferences, you can offer relevant recommendations, leading to additional sales.

3. **Referral Generation**: Satisfied customers are more likely to refer your business to friends, family, or colleagues. A strong follow-up can encourage customers to spread positive word-of-mouth, generating new leads and potential sales.

4. **Customer Feedback and Improvement**: Following up allows you to gather valuable customer feedback about their experience with your product or service. This feedback can help you identify areas for improvement, refine your offerings, and enhance the overall customer experience.

5. **Brand Reputation and Trust**: A prompt and attentive follow-up builds trust and enhances your brand reputation. When customers feel valued and supported even after the sale, they are more likely to view your business as reliable and trustworthy, leading to increased sales and positive brand perception.

6. **Competitive Advantage**: A strong follow-up can differentiate your business from competitors in today's competitive market. By providing exceptional customer service and maintaining a

connection, you stand out as a genuinely caring business, giving you an edge in securing future sales.

A strong follow-up with customers is essential for nurturing relationships, driving repeat business, generating referrals, gathering feedback, and establishing a positive brand reputation. It is an investment in the long-term success and growth of your business.

CHAPTER 11

THE EVOLUTION OF FIRST IMPRESSIONS:

FROM IN-PERSON TO ONLINE

"First impressions matter. Experts say we size up new people in somewhere between 30 seconds and two minutes."

\- Elliott Abrams

Elliott Abrams, a renowned psychologist, emphasizes the importance of first impressions. Years ago, these impressions were formed during in-person introductions. Today, however, the landscape has shifted dramatically, with first impressions often being made online. This chapter explores the evolution of first impressions, the importance of verbal and non-verbal cues, and how the digital age, accelerated by the COVID-19 pandemic, has transformed how we meet, date, and do business.

Section 1: The Importance of In-Person Introductions

In-person introductions have been, and continue to be, a crucial aspect of human interaction. The verbal exchange of greetings and the non-verbal cues, such as body language, eye contact, and facial expressions, all form first impressions. These impressions can significantly influence personal relationships and business dealings.

Section 2: The Shift to Online First Impressions

With the advent of the digital age, first impressions have increasingly moved online. Social media profiles, online reviews, and digital interactions now play a significant role in shaping perceptions.

Whether it's a business being evaluated based on its online reviews or an individual being considered for a date based on their social media profile, the online persona has become a critical determinant of first impressions.

Section 3: The Impact of Verbal and Non-Verbal Cues Online

Just as in-person interactions rely on verbal and non-verbal cues, so do online interactions. The words we choose, the tone we use, and even the timing of our responses can shape perceptions. Similarly, non-verbal cues such as the images we post, the aesthetics of our website, or the emojis we use can also influence how we are perceived.

Section 4: The Influence of COVID-19

The COVID-19 pandemic has further accelerated the shift towards online interactions. With physical distancing measures in place, more people have turned to online platforms for meeting, dating, and doing business. This shift has underscored the importance of managing our online presence and ensuring that our digital-first impressions are as strong as our in-person ones.

Section 5: The Importance of Both In-Person and Online Impressions

Despite the shift towards online interactions, in-person introductions remain essential. As society reopens post-pandemic, online and in-person interactions will blend. Therefore, it's crucial to master both forms of introductions. Whether maintaining eye contact during an in-person meeting or crafting a compelling online profile, both are essential in shaping positive first impressions.

Conclusion:

First impressions have evolved from being primarily in-person to increasingly online. However, the core principles remain the same. Whether in-person or online, how we present ourselves verbally and non-verbally can significantly influence our perception.

In the post-COVID era, mastering both introductions is more crucial than ever as we navigate a blend of online and in-person interactions. By understanding and adapting to this evolution, we can ensure that our first impressions, whether in-person or online, are positive and impactful.

CHAPTER 12

NAVIGATING THE DIGITAL LANDSCAPE:

SEPARATING PERSONAL AND PROFESSIONAL LIVES

In the evolving landscape of human interaction, where in-person meetings have given way to online interactions, managing our perceived image has become more critical than ever. The impressions we make online can significantly impact our personal and professional lives. Therefore, it's crucial to maintain a clear distinction between the two, preventing any misjudgments or misconceptions that could deter us from our goals and aspirations. This chapter will provide practical suggestions on how to keep personal and professional lives separate in the digital realm.

Section 1: The Importance of Separation

The intertwining of personal and professional lives online can lead to many complications. Personal opinions or activities can be misconstrued, leading to potential professional repercussions. By keeping these two aspects of life separate, we can ensure that our professional image remains untarnished and our personal lives remain private.

Section 2: Practical Suggestions for Separation

1. **Separate Social Media Accounts**: Consider having separate social media accounts for personal and professional purposes. This allows you to share professional updates and engage with colleagues or clients on one platform while keeping your personal life private on another.

2. **Privacy Settings**: Make use of the privacy settings on social media platforms. These settings can help control who sees your posts, ensuring that personal content is only visible to those you trust.

3. **Professional Email Address**: Use a professional email address for all business-related communications. This helps maintain a professional image and keeps your personal email separate.

4. **Be Mindful of What You Share**: Always think before you post. Consider how your post could be perceived by others, especially those in your professional network.

5. **Online Etiquette**: Maintain a respectful and professional tone in all online interactions. Avoid engaging in online arguments or sharing controversial opinions that could harm your professional image.

Conclusion:

The lines between our personal and professional lives can often blur in the digital age. However, we can maintain a clear distinction between the two by taking proactive steps. This helps prevent any potential misjudgments or misconceptions and allows us to present a consistent and professional image online. Keeping our personal and professional lives separate will be key to achieving our goals and aspirations as we continue to navigate this new interaction evolution.

CHAPTER 13

THE POWER OF CUSTOMER SERVICE IN THE DIGITAL AGE USING VERBAL AND NON-VERBAL COMMUNICATION

In the ever-evolving landscape of human interaction, the importance of customer service remains a constant. From in-person interactions to social media engagements, the power of verbal and non-verbal communication in delivering exceptional customer service cannot be overstated.

In the digital age, customer service has taken on new dimensions. It's no longer confined to face-to-face interactions or phone conversations. Today, it extends to social media platforms, online reviews, and email exchanges. Despite the medium change, effective communication principles remain the same.

Verbal communication, whether it's the words we choose or the tone we use, can significantly impact a customer's experience. Similarly, non-verbal cues, such as response time on social media or the user-friendliness of a website, also play a crucial role in shaping customer perceptions.

Consistency is key to delivering exceptional customer service. From the first interaction to the last, and even after, maintaining a consistent level of service helps build trust and fosters customer loyalty. It's about ensuring that every touchpoint, whether in person or online, reflects your commitment to customer satisfaction.

As we navigate this new era of customer service, we must be willing to adapt and evolve. Embracing change, leveraging new technologies, and continually refining our communication strategies are crucial for success.

In the words of Charles Darwin, *"It is not the strongest of the species that survives, nor the most intelligent; it is the one most adaptable to change."* This quote holds true in the realm of customer service. Our ability to adapt will determine our success in a world where change is the only constant.

In conclusion, the power of customer service, underpinned by effective verbal and non-verbal communication, is a critical driver of success today. From in-person interactions to social media engagements, maintaining consistency and adapting to change are essential. As we continue to navigate the digital landscape, let us remember that at the heart of every interaction is a customer who values being heard, understood, and appreciated.

CHAPTER 14

THE FOUNDATION
OF VISION:

UNVEILING PURPOSE AND GOALS

In the realm of serving others, it is crucial to establish a solid foundation before we embark on the journey of posting and serving. This chapter examines the significance of crafting a clear vision and purpose as the starting point for a new venture. We will explore the power of vision, the importance of defining purpose, and how thought-provoking questions can guide us in creating a compelling vision and purpose.

Section 1: The Power of Vision

A vision acts as a guiding star, illuminating our path and inspiring us to take action. It is the seed from which our goals and aspirations grow. Before effectively serving others, we must first envision the impact we wish to make. As Helen Keller once said, *"The only thing worse than being blind is having sight but no vision."* A vision gives us direction, clarity, and a sense of purpose.

Section 2: Defining Purpose

The purpose is the driving force behind our actions. It is the deep-rooted reason why we embark on a new venture. To uncover our purpose, we must reflect on our passions, values, and the impact we desire to create. What ignites our enthusiasm? What change do we want to bring to the world? By understanding our purpose, we align our actions with our values and find fulfillment in serving others.

Section 3: Thought-Provoking Questions

Creating a compelling vision and purpose requires introspection and exploration. Here are some thought-provoking questions to guide us on this journey:

1. What inspires me? Reflect on the experiences, people, or causes that ignite your passion and drive.
2. What are my core values? Identify the principles and beliefs that guide your decisions and actions.
3. What impact do I want to make? Envision the change you wish to bring to the world and the lives of others.
4. Who do I want to serve? Define your target audience and understand their needs, desires, and challenges.
5. How can I leverage my strengths? Identify your unique skills, talents, and expertise that can contribute to your vision.

Section 4: Crafting a Compelling Vision and Purpose

Armed with the insights gained from self-reflection and answering thought-provoking questions, we can craft a compelling vision and purpose. A vision statement should be concise, inspiring, and future-oriented. It should encapsulate the impact we want to create and serve as a guiding light. As we embark on this journey, let us remember the words of Walt Disney, who said, "All our dreams can come true if we dare to pursue them."

Conclusion:

A strong vision and purpose lay the groundwork for a successful venture in serving others. By reflecting on our passions, values, and desired impact, we can create a compelling vision that inspires us and resonates with our target audience.

Thought-provoking questions serve as a compass, guiding us toward uncovering our purpose and aligning our actions with our deepest aspirations. As we move forward, let us embrace the power of vision and purpose, knowing that they are the driving forces behind our journey of posting and serving others.

SUGGESTIONS OF BOOKS TO READ

Here are some excellent books that delve into creating raving fans, providing exceptional customer service, and leveraging social media for business growth:

1. **"Raving Fans: A Revolutionary Approach to Customer Service" by Ken Blanchard and Sheldon Bowles**: This book provides a new approach to customer service, suggesting that simply satisfying customers is not enough, and businesses should aim to create 'raving fans' who are so impressed that they tell others about their experience.

2. **"Delivering Happiness: A Path to Profits, Passion, and Purpose" by Tony Hsieh:** The CEO of Zappos shares his insights on how focusing on company culture and customer service can lead to success.

3. **"The Thank You Economy" by Gary Vaynerchuk**: This book emphasizes the importance of social media in business and how it has changed the way we communicate with customers.

4. **"Hug Your Haters: How to Embrace Complaints and Keep Your Customers" by Jay Baer**: This book provides a new

perspective on customer complaints and how businesses can use them to their advantage.

5. **"The Art of Social Media: Power Tips for Power Users" by Guy Kawasaki and Peg Fitzpatrick**: This book offers practical tips and strategies for businesses to effectively use social media to engage with customers and grow their brand.

6. **"Made to Stick: Why Some Ideas Survive, and Others Die" by Chip Heath and Dan Heath**: This book explores why some ideas become popular while others don't, offering valuable insights for businesses looking to create a memorable brand.

7. **"Influence: The Psychology of Persuasion" by Robert Cialdini**: This book delves into the psychology behind why people say 'yes' and how to apply these insights in real-world situations, including customer service.

8. **"Never Lose a Customer Again: Turn Any Sale into Lifelong Loyalty in 100 Days" by Joey Coleman**: This book provides a step-by-step guide to improving customer loyalty and reducing churn.

9. **"Crushing It: How Great Entrepreneurs Build Their Business and Influence—and How You Can, too" by Gary Vaynerchuk**: This book shares success stories of entrepreneurs who have grown their businesses through social media and personal branding.

10. **"The Power of Moments: Why Certain Experiences Have Extraordinary Impact" by Chip Heath and Dan Heath**: This book explores how to create memorable, impactful experiences that can transform customer relationships.

These books offer a wealth of knowledge and practical advice on creating raving fans, delivering exceptional customer service, and leveraging social media for business growth.

Contact Information

If you have any questions, would like to schedule an interview, or wish to inquire about booking Giulio Veglio for a speaking event, please feel free to get in touch through the following channels:

Website: http://www.giulioveglio.com
Email: talkvisionary@gmail.com

We look forward to hearing from you and discussing how Giulio Veglio's books can impact your readers or event.

www.ingramcontent.com/pod-product-compliance
Lightning Source LLC
Chambersburg PA
CBHW051233120626
46547CB00013B/1626

* 9 7 8 1 9 6 3 2 5 0 7 8 7 *